The Sun is Broken

Andrés Pi Andreu
Illustrated by Catty Flores

Play Station 1

 1 **Listen and point.**

(A)

(B)

(C)

(D)

(E)

(F)

(G)

(H)

(I)

2 **Match the words and the pictures in ①.**

◯ party food	◯ game	◯ birthday cake
◯ present	◯ candles	◯ toys
◯ birthday card	◯ balloons	◯ music

3 **Listen. Say the chant. Then read and match.**

A "It's my birthday." "Here's a present. Here's a present."

B "It's my birthday." "Here's a card. Here's a card."

C "It's my birthday." "Come, let's play. Come, let's play."

D "It's my birthday." "Here's a cake. Here's a cake."

E "It's my birthday." "Make a wish. Make a wish."

F "It's my birthday." "Now let's eat. Now let's eat."

4 **Listen and mime.**

 5 **Listen and write the numbers.**

 6 **Look and write.**

A The little girl has got a hat and a dress.

B Mum has ....

C Dad ....

7 **Listen and match.**

A a red dress

B blue trousers

C big blue eyes

D an orange and white top

E a purple and pink hat

F long black hair

8 **Look at ⑤ and tell a friend.**

> She's got a purple and pink party hat.

> She's got big blue eyes.

9 **Look at a friend. Say.**

> You've got .... hair.

> You've got .... trousers.

5

Today is the little girl's birthday. There is a big birthday cake with seven candles.

"Happy Birthday," say Mum and Dad.
"Now, blow out the candles and make a wish."

The little girl blows and she blows and she blows. Then she makes a wish.

What can a fire-fighting mailcow do?
Match and draw lines.

A fight   mail

B deliver   fires

The little girl runs to the window.
There's a fire-fighting mailcow.
It's flying in the sky.
"Maybe it's got a birthday card from Grandma,"
says the little girl.

Think of another farm animal. Tick (✓).

☐ It makes milk.
☐ It can fly.
☐ It's got wings.

But the little girl knows that it *is* a cow.
A fire-fighting mailcow for her birthday.

"Woof! Woof!" says Buster the dog.
He wants to sing 'Happy Birthday'
to the little girl.

"Dad," says the little girl.
"Buster wants to sing 'Happy Birthday'."

"Don't be silly, little one. Dogs can't sing,"
says Dad. And he reads his newspaper.

"Hello?" says the little girl on the phone.
"Mum! Dad! Grandma Matilda is on the phone.
She is calling to wish me a happy birthday!"

Answer the phone. What do you say?

"Darling, Grandma Matilda is dead.
She lives in the sky, now," says Mum.
"There are no phones in the sky," says Dad.
And Mum and Dad hug the little girl.

The little girl is sad now.
She looks out of the window at the sky.

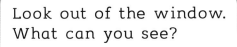

Look out of the window.
What can you see?

Tell a friend.

Then, she has an idea.
"Wow! Where is her house?
How does she get there?"
asks the little girl.

Draw a cloud bus and a rocket taxi. Show a friend.

"On a cloud bus?
Or a rocket taxi?
Or maybe she's got
a special plane."

Dad takes the little girl's hand and they walk outside. "Look, my little one. The sun is going down. Look at the beautiful sunset."

Dad wants to talk to the little girl about the sun and the sky and Grandma.
But the little girl says:

Dad!
The sun
is broken!

Close your eyes.
Think of the sunset.
What colours can you see?

Then half of the sun falls into the sea.
It makes a big splash and all
the colours melt into the water.

Colour and write.

What colours make orange?

⬜ + ⬜ = 🟧

.... + ... = orange

What colours make purple?

⬜ + ⬜ = 🟪

.... + ... = purple

The little girl's
parents can't
believe their eyes.
They stand at the
window, looking
at the sun.

The little girl smiles,
she can see Grandma
and her special plane
and the mailcow.

Point to the things the little girl can see.

What do you think? Can Mum and Dad see the things, too?

Play Station 2

1 **Look, read and tick (✔) the correct sentence.**

A ⭕ The little girl blows out the candles on her birthday cake.

⭕ The little girl eats her birthday cake.

B ⭕ The little girl thinks about Grandma Matilda.

⭕ The little girl thinks about her parents.

C ⭕ Dad talks to the little girl in the morning.

⭕ Dad talks to the little girl in the evening.

2 **Find your favourite picture from the story. Show a friend.**

3 **Complete the sentences with the correct verbs.**

A Today .... the little girl's birthday.

B The little girl .... a wish.

C The little girl .... to the window.

D The little girl .... it is a mailcow.

E Dad .... his newspaper.

F Grandma Matilda .... in the sky.

G Dad .... the little girl's hand.

H Half of the sun .... into the sea.

takes
runs
reads
lives
falls
makes
knows
is

4 **Look at the pictures. Write the words.**

A _ _ _ _ _ _   T E N S S U

B _ _ _ _ _ _ _ _ _   P R E W N S P A E

C _ _ _ _ _   E N P O H

D _ _ _ _ _ _   T K R C O E

E _ _ _ _ _ _   D I W N O W

Play Station 2

5 **Match the words and pictures.**

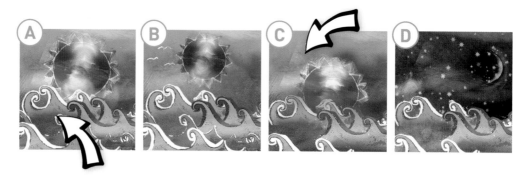

◯ night   ◯ morning   ◯ evening   ◯ afternoon

6 **Listen, say the poem and mime.**

Good morning. Good morning.
The sun wakes up.
Good afternoon. Good afternoon.
The sun shines in the sky.
Good evening. Good evening.
The sun goes down.
Good night. Good night.
It's time to sleep.

7 **Read and circle.**

A The little girl wake / wakes up in the morning.

B The little girl plays / play in the afternoon.

C The little girl go / goes to bed in the evening.

D The little girl sleeps / sleep at night.

8 **Listen and check.**

9 **What do you do? Ask and tell a friend.**

What do you do in the morning?

I wake up in the morning.

Play Station 2

10 **Read and circle.**

A Cows can / can't fly.

B Cows can / can't make milk.

C Dogs can / can't sing.

D Firefighters can / can't fight fires.

E Mailmen can / can't deliver birthday cards.

F Dad can / can't read the newspaper.

11 **Look and match.**

○  ○  ○  ○

A He can draw. B They can write. C She can read. D It can fly.

12 **Write and tell a friend.**

One thing I can do. ☺   One thing I can't do. ☹

....

....

....

13 **Read, look and write.**

I've got four .... ,

two ears, two eyes and a long ....

I don't live in a .... or a garden.

I like eating ....

I drink .... I make ....

I can also deliver ....

and fight ....

I have .... and I can fly.

What am I? I'm a fire-fighting mailcow.

14 **Listen and check.**

15 **Think of an animal. Mime and tell a friend.**

Play Station Project

Phones

Make a metal can phone.

You need:

2 clean and dry
metal food cans

a long piece
of string

1 Ask an adult to make
a small hole in the
bottom of the cans.

2 Put some of the string
through the hole
(from the outside).
Tie two small knots
with the string
inside the can.

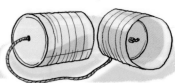

3 Repeat step **2**
with the other can
and the other end
of the piece of string.

Ring,
ring.
Ring,
ring.

Hello.

Hello, can I speak to ... ?

Speaking. Who's calling?

It's ... .

Hi, how are you?

I'm fine, thanks. And you?

Well, thanks.

Can you hear me?

Yes!

Great! This phone works. Bye!

Bye!

Ring,
ring.

4 One person talks into one of the cans.
The other person holds the other can to his
or her ear to listen. Remember! The string must
be tight/straight for the sound to travel.

Go to www.helblingyoungreaders.com to download this page.